ALLIGATORS AND CROCODILES

ALLIGATORS AND CROCODILES

MICHAEL GEORGE

THE CHILD'S WORLD

DESIGN
Bill Foster of Albarella & Associates, Inc.

PHOTO CREDITS
Tom and Pat Leeson: front cover, 17, 26
Susan Petterson: back cover
Frank Todd/Ecosystems International: 2, 15
Len Rue Jr.: 6, 8, 25
Leonard Rue III: 8(inset), 18
Joe McDonald: 10, 12, 28
Ralph A. Clevenger: 20
W. Perry Conway: 22, 30

Distributed to schools and libraries
in the United States by

ENCYCLOPAEDIA BRITANNICA EDUCATIONAL CORP

310 South Michigan Ave.
Chicago, Illinois 60604

Library of Congress Cataloging-in-Publication Data
George, Michael, 1964-
Alligators and Crocodiles/Michael George
p. cm. — (Child's World Wildlife Library)
Summary: Describes the characteristics, habitat, behavior, and
life cycle of alligators and crocodiles.
ISBN 0-89565-720-1
1. Alligators — Juvenile literature.   2. Crocodiles — Juvenile literature.
[1. Alligators.   2. Crocodiles.]   I. Title.
II. Series.   91-13480
QL666.C925G46 1991   CIP
597.98—dc20   AC

Dedicated to Dave and Steph

Do alligators and crocodiles remind you of dragons? If so, you are not alone. Like the legendary dragon, alligators and crocodiles are covered by tough, scaly hides. They also have long tails, clawed feet, and huge, tooth-filled mouths. Although they cannot fly or breathe fire, alligators and crocodiles do have one advantage over the mighty dragon. Dragons are found only in books, movies, and bad dreams. Alligators and crocodiles are real!

Although they look very much alike, alligators and crocodiles are different in several ways. Crocodiles have slender bodies and long, pointed snouts. Alligators, on the other hand, have stockier bodies and wide, blunt snouts.

Appearance is not the only difference between crocodiles and alligators. Much like the mythical dragon, crocodiles are fearsome, man-eating beasts. They have been known to stalk and eat people. Alligators are not nearly so dangerous. Normally, they are shy and stay away from humans.

Crocodile

Inset: Alligator

There are two different kinds of alligators, Chinese and American. Chinese alligators live on the eastern coast of China. In the wild, they grow to about 10 feet long. American alligators live only in the southeastern United States. The largest American alligators can grow to more than 15 feet long.

Alligators spend most of their lives in swamps, ponds, or rivers. An alligator swims by swinging its long tail from side to side. Its webbed feet also help the alligator paddle through the water. An adult alligator can swim about six miles per hour. That's as fast as a small motorboat!

Although they are fast swimmers, alligators usually drift slowly through the water, barely visible above the surface. An alligator's eyes and nostrils are on the top of its snout. This enables the alligator to see and breathe while its body is hidden underwater. When the alligator dives, special muscles close its nose and ears. In addition, clear eyelids — like swimming goggles — slide down over its eyes. Thus protected, an alligator can stay underwater for over an hour.

Alligators are not picky eaters. They like to snack on snakes, birds, fish, and frogs. Alligators also eat mice, muskrats, turtles, and rabbits. Large alligators sometimes attack pigs, deer, and even cattle. Although people are not on their menu, alligators have been known to eat unleashed dogs.

Adult alligators have up to 80 teeth in their gaping mouths. The largest teeth can be more than three inches long. However, none of the teeth are used for chewing. The alligator swallows its food in one gulp, bones and all. If an animal is too big to be swallowed all at once, the alligator tears its meal into smaller pieces.

Fortunately for their victims, alligators eat only about once a week. Alligators don't eat very often because they don't have to. Alligators are cold-blooded — their body temperature is always the same as their surroundings. As a result, they do not have to waste energy keeping their bodies warm. If they get cold, alligators simply warm themselves in the sun.

In March, adult alligators search for mates. They call to each other with eerie, bellowing roars. About three weeks after mating, female alligators build nests. They usually pick an isolated place that is close to the water. They use their hind feet to pile up grass, plants, and sand.

After her nest is completed, a female alligator lays between 30 and 60 baseball-sized eggs. About two months later, the baby alligators chip their way out of their shells. When they emerge, the baby alligators, called *hatchlings*, are only about nine inches long. They immediately make their way to the water. Few, if any, ever see their mother again.

The hatchlings begin to search for food when they are about three days old. They eat insects, minnows, frogs, and anything else they can catch. As they look for food, the hatchlings must be very careful. Many creatures think that a tiny alligator makes a tasty snack!

If they are not gobbled up by larger enemies, the little hatchlings grow quickly. After about four years, they are about four feet long. By now, the young alligators are covered with thick, tough scales like the grown-ups. The alligators' hides protect them from sharp rocks as they glide through the water. The tough scales also protect the alligators from their former enemies.

No longer threatened by other swampland creatures, the young alligators are now adults. Other adult alligators are no longer willing to share their ponds. Alligators open their mouths and hiss when another adult comes too close. If the intruder doesn't leave, there could be a fierce and bloody battle.

Nile Crocodile

Driven out by larger adults, the young alligators journey overland in search of their own swamps or ponds. On land, alligators normally move slowly, with their bodies close to the ground. If threatened, however, they lift up their bodies and scurry across the ground. At full speed, and adult alligator can run faster than you can!

Eventually, each young alligator finds a swamp or pond to call its own. Here, the alligator suns itself peacefully or drifts quietly through the water. Like the legendary dragon, the mighty alligator knows it is the king of its watery domain.